MAT MAN

OPPOSITES

By Jan Z. Olsen • Illustrations by Molly Delaney

8001 MacArthur Blvd
Cabin John, MD 20818
888.983.8409
LWTears.com

Printed in Hong Kong

First Edition
ISBN: 978-1-891627-94-1
101112REGAL201918

Mat Man stands.

stand

Mat Man sits.
Let's say opposites.

sit

He says smile.

smile

You say frown.

frown

He says up.

up

You say down.

down

Mat Man stands.

stand

Mat Man sits.
Let's say opposites.

sit

He says whisper.

whisper

You say
shout.

shout

He says in.

in

You say out.

out

He says wet.

wet

You say dry.

dry

He says laugh.

laugh

You say cry.

cry

Mat Man stands.

stand

Mat Man sits.
Let's say opposites.

sit

He says push.

push

You say pull.

pull

He says empty.

empty

You say full.

full

He says old.

old

You say new.

new

He says many.

many

You say few.

few

Mat Man stands.

stand

Mat Man sits.
Let's say opposites.

sit

He says real.

real

You say pretend.

pretend

He says start.

start

You say end.

end

Opposites are everywhere.

See if you can find a pair.